Hunting and Fishing

Kyle Brach

Lerner Publications ◆ Minneapolis

Copyright © 2024 by Lerner Publishing Group, Inc.

All rights reserved. International copyright secured. No part of this book may be reproduced, stored in a retrieval system, or transmitted in any form or by any means—electronic, mechanical, photocopying, recording, or otherwise—without the prior written permission of Lerner Publishing Group, Inc., except for the inclusion of brief quotations in an acknowledged review.

Lerner Publications Company
An imprint of Lerner Publishing Group, Inc.
241 First Avenue North
Minneapolis, MN 55401 USA

For reading levels and more information, look up this title at www.lernerbooks.com.

Main body text set in Adrianna Regular.
Typeface provided by Chank.

Library of Congress Cataloging-in-Publication Data

Names: Brach, Kyle, author.
Title: Big game hunting / Kyle Brach.
Description: Minneapolis, MN, USA : Lerner Publications Company, an imprint of Lerner Publishing Group, Inc., [2024] | Series: Searchlight books. Hunting and fishing | Includes bibliographical references and index. | Audience: Ages 8-11 | Audience: Grades 4-6 | Summary: "Big game hunting is hunting for large animals such as moose. From the needed equipment to hunting safely, readers will learn all they should and would want to know about big game hunting"— Provided by publisher.
Identifiers: LCCN 2022050002 (print) | LCCN 2022050003 (ebook) | ISBN 9781728491523 (lib. bdg.) | ISBN 9798765603710 (pbk.) | ISBN 9798765600276 (eb pdf)
Subjects: LCSH: Big game hunting—Juvenile literature.
Classification: LCC SK35.5 .B73 2024 (print) | LCC SK35.5 (ebook) | DDC 799.2/6—dc23/eng/20221116

LC record available at https://lccn.loc.gov/2022050002
LC ebook record available at https://lccn.loc.gov/2022050003

Manufactured in the United States of America
1 - CG - 7/15/2023

Table of Contents

Chapter 1
BIG GAME ANIMALS AND YOUR GEAR . . . 4

Chapter 2
SAFE HUNTING PRACTICES . . . 14

Chapter 3
HUNTING BASICS . . . 20

Chapter 4
CONSERVATION . . . 26

Glossary • 30
Learn More • 31
Index • 32

Chapter 1

BIG GAME ANIMALS AND YOUR GEAR

Way up in a tree, you remain motionless in your stand. Your nose itches, but you don't dare scratch it. You hear rustling leaves. You scan the woods, looking for any movement. Look! Just ahead! What you thought was a shadow is a black bear foraging for food. It comes into the open briefly, and you have your first clear shot. You aim . . . and fire!

What Is Big Game?

Big game hunting provides a level of excitement few outdoor activities can rival. You're matching wits with animals that are fast, smart, and huge! And you're on their turf. It takes skill, courage, and experience to hunt white-tailed deer, moose, elk, black bears, wild boar, and other big game animals.

Black bears are popular big game prey sought by hunters.

Popular Big Game Animals

The most popular game in the US, the white-tailed deer, can be found in most states and in Canada. Mule deer are popular to hunt as well. They have long ears, like a mule, and can be found in the Rocky Mountains, the Pacific Northwest, and in the Southwest deserts.

Tail flagging alerts other deer in the herd of danger.

Hunting History

As early European settlers made their way west, many big game animals in the US were overhunted to the point of near extinction. These included elk, pronghorn, and bison. In 1804 the Lewis and Clark expedition killed 374 elk during their two-year journey. Hunting was not yet regulated. By the early 1900s the elk population plummeted from ten million to fifty thousand. After years of regulations and conservation, the elk population is up to one million.

Conservation efforts helped save elk from extinction.

THE SHAWNEE AND CREE NATIONS CALLED ELK WAPITI, MEANING WHITE RUMP.

More Big Game Animals

The moose is one of the biggest land animals in North America, weighing 1,100 pounds (499 kg) or more. Male moose have massive antlers. They live in forests with lakes and swamps in the northern US and Canada.

Elk prefer steep, forested environments, and can weigh 800 pounds (362.9 kg) or more. The males also have big antlers, and they can be found in the western US and Canada.

Black bears live mostly in forests in the East and in forests and wooded mountains in the West, where they can be cinnamon- or chocolate-colored. They have an amazing sense of smell and can sniff out humans from over a mile away! They can also climb trees and run up to 35 miles (56.3 km) per hour.

Other big game that can be hunted include wild hogs, pronghorn, bighorn sheep, and woodland caribou.

Moose are great swimmers!

Hunting with Guns

Whether you are tracking an elk on the ground or waiting for a deer in a tree stand, you'll want to have the right firearm and gear with you.

RIFLE SCOPES HELP YOU AIM TO GET A MORE PRECISE SHOT.

Hunter loading a single-shot rifle

Most hunters hunt for big game with a rifle, which shoots bullets and has a long barrel with grooves on the inside. For young hunters, it is important to find a gun you can handle that is also appropriate for big game. If your rifle is too powerful, you'll end up hurting yourself. If it's not powerful enough, you may only injure an animal. It's best to try several models at a shooting range before choosing.

Some experienced hunters use compound bows to hunt big game.

Hunting with a Bow and Arrows

It takes strength, skill, and patience to hunt big game with a bow and arrow. Big game hunters use a compound bow, which is a system of pulleys, wheels, and strings that makes pulling back the bowstring easier. This produces a fast and powerful shot. Bowhunters need to get closer to their game because arrows don't travel as far as bullets. You need to be an experienced hunter to get close to big game animals.

THE POINT OF BIG GAME ARROWS IS CALLED A BROADHEAD, WHICH WILL HAVE TWO OR MORE SHARP STEEL BLADES.

Other Equipment

Along with your firearm or bow, you should have binoculars, a first aid kit, a sharp knife, a compass, and a flashlight.

Chapter 2

SAFE HUNTING PRACTICES

The best way to be safe out in the wild is to know how to use your weapon. Take the required classes, practice on stationary targets at ranges, and get advice from experienced hunters.

Only put your finger on the trigger when you are ready to shoot.

Gun Safety

There are four basic rules for gun safety. Act as if every gun you handle is loaded. Be sure to point your weapon in a safe direction and never point it at other people. Only shoot at targets when you are certain there is nothing in front or behind it. And keep your finger off the trigger until you are ready to shoot.

Dress in layers and make sure you have lots of pockets for snacks. Backpacks are used to bring safety supplies and other gear.

Dress for Safety Success

When dressing for hunting, you want to keep three things in mind: the weather, noise, and other hunters.

Dress for the worst weather that could happen the day you go hunting. It may be warm at your house, but in the woods, it may be colder and damper. Dressing in layers gives you options as temperatures change during the day.

Most animals have a great sense of hearing. If you're rustling around in your nylon jacket, there's a chance you'll be going home empty-handed. Wear soft clothes that give you room to move.

Camouflage helps you blend into the environment where you are hunting. But you also need to be aware of other hunters. That's why you must wear bright orange vests, hats, and more. Hunters won't mistake you for game, and many animals can't see orange because they are red-green colorblind.

Hunters wearing blaze orange clothing are easily seen by other hunters.

Other Safety Considerations

Keeping things safe for you and others includes staying clear of other hunters, never hunting alone, and always being aware of your surroundings. Also, the animals you are hunting are dangerous. Know about the animals you are hunting as well as other animals you might come across.

It is wise to never get between a mama bear and her cubs.

STEM Spotlight

Male deer (including elk and moose) grow antlers. Antlers are made of solid bone and are covered with a soft, thin layer of skin and blood vessels that gets scraped off over time. Antlers are shed every year. Horns are hollow bones covered in keratin. It's what human fingernails are made of. Both male and female bison, goats, and pronghorn have permanent horns.

Both male and female reindeer have antlers.

Chapter 3

HUNTING BASICS

When hunting big game, you must think like they do. You are at a disadvantage because you are on their territory. This is part of what makes hunting such a fun challenge for millions of people a year.

Learn what the animal you're hunting eats and when and where it likes to eat. Learn what its scat (poop) looks like. One way to do this is to scout your hunting location ahead of time. It's like being a detective on a hike. Instead of looking for evidence to catch a criminal, you are looking for anything that indicates game has been there. Scat, tracks, and flattened ground used for resting are all clues.

Elk like grassy meadows but will seek higher ground in wooded areas if they sense danger.

Hunt into the wind so game doesn't catch your scent.

Still Hunting

For some big game, it is best to be on the move. When still-hunting, the slower you move, the better. Each step is thought out and careful, and you avoid breaking sticks or rustling leaves. Be sure to hunt downwind so your scent doesn't warn prey away.

When still-hunting, it's very important your clothes don't make any noise. Stay in the shade when possible, and use trees, bushes, and boulders to hide.

Hunting by canoe adds more challenge to the sport.

Stands and Blinds

Instead of moving around, you can stay in one place and wait. To do that, you'll need a good hiding place. That's where stands and blinds can be helpful.

Stands are platforms attached to trees that are 10 to 15 feet (3 to 4.6 m) above ground. From up there, big game won't immediately see or smell you. This height gives you an advantage.

This blind is camouflaged to fool animals.

Blinds are human-made camouflaged tents where you can remain unseen on the ground. Natural blinds can be thick bushes, a log, or a hill where you can see but not be seen.

Make sure to place your blind or stand close to game food sources, watering holes, or trails. Scout before you decide where to wait for prey.

Know how to set up your tree stand before you take it into the woods.

Chapter 4

CONSERVATION

Hunters want to preserve habitats and animal populations so they can enjoy hunting for years to come. To conserve something is to prevent it from being wasted. Hunters do many things to make sure we are wisely conserving our natural resources.

▲
NEVER HUNT ON PRIVATE LANDS WITHOUT PERMISSION.

Hunters spend more money and time on wildlife conservation than any other group. Hunters pay for licenses, permits, and tags (which you place on hunted animals), as well as government-funded training programs. This money goes right back into making sure animals and their habitats are protected.

Hunters Follow the Rules

Hunting without a license is illegal and can lead to animals being overhunted. Hunters pay attention to the different hunting seasons. They know what they can hunt and when. Good hunters also preserve natural habitats by not littering or cutting branches from trees to make blinds.

Without conservation, there would be little to no hunting. Hunters love what they do and want to protect it for generations to come.

Without game protection laws, many species, such as pronghorn, would have gone extinct.

Hunting Hints

- Place your blind downwind or crosswind of where you expect to see prey.

- Pay attention to the difference between fresh tracks and old ones. Fresh tracks have clearly defined edges.

- Stalk potential game to get closer. Move slowly into shooting range so you are in position for a good shot.

- Another way to hunt is called glassing, where you sit from a vantage point until you spot game. Then, you stalk it.

Glossary

blind: human-made or natural camouflaged shelter for hunters to hide in while waiting for game

camouflage: a type of clothing made with a green and brown pattern that helps hunters blend into their natural surroundings

conservation: to carefully protect nature

extinction: a situation in which a species of animal no longer exists

game: animals pursued in hunting

habitat: where a plant or animal naturally lives

rifle: a gun with a long barrel with spiral grooves on its inside

season: a period of the year when it is allowed to hunt specific types of game

stand: a platform secured to a tree for hunters to stand on or sit in

Learn More

Bailey, Diane. *Small Game Hunting*. Minneapolis: Lerner Publications, 2024.

Brach, Kyle. *Bowhunting*. Minneapolis: Lerner Publications, 2024.

Doyle, Abby Badach. *Big Game Hunting*. New York: Gareth Stevens Publishing, 2023.

Easy Science for Kids: Wild Deer
https://easyscienceforkids.com/all-about-deer

Kiddle: Big-Game Hunting Facts for Kids
https://kids.kiddle.co/Big-game_hunting

SoftSchools: Hunting Facts
https://www.softschools.com/facts/sports/hunting_facts/2748/

Index

blind, 24–25, 28–29

bow and arrow, 12–13

clothing, 16–17

conservation, 26, 28

gear, 10, 16

gun safety, 15

license, 27–28

scout, 21, 25

stand, 4, 10, 24–25

still hunting, 22–23

Photo Acknowledgments

Image Credits: p.5; KenCanning/iStock Photos, p. 6; Steve Oehlenschlager/Shutterstock, p. 7; Harry Collins Photography/Shutterstock, p. 8; Steve Meese/Shutterstock, p. 9; Frontpage/Shutterstock, p. 10; jfwalker/Shutterstock, p. 11; Andrey Merenov/Dreamstime, p. 12; REDAV/Shutterstock, p. 13; Olga Popova/Shutterstock, p. 15; Volodymyr TVERDOKHLIB/Shutterstock, p. 16; saz1977/iStock Photos, p. 17; iheartcountryphoto/Dreamstime, p. 18; jo Crebbin/Shutterstock, p. 19; Dennis Welker/iStock Photos, p. 21; Mark A Lee/Shutterstock, p. 22; Roman Kosolapov/Shutterstock, p. 23; Phillip W Kirkland/Shutterstock, p. 24; Robert Wedderburn/Shutterstock, p. 25; Stephen Oehlenschlager/Dreamstime, p. 27; Sketchart/Shutterstock, p. 28; Kyle Spadley Photography/Shutterstock.

Cover: Dan Martin/Dreamstime.